FORTUNE COOKIE

JENNA CLAKE

FORTUNE COOKIE

▭▭ EYEWEAR PUBLISHING

First published in 2017
by Eyewear Publishing Ltd
Suite 333, 19-21 Crawford Street
Marylebone, London W1H 1PJ
United Kingdom

Cover design and typeset by Edwin Smet
Author photograph by Lauren Birch
Printed in England by TJ International Ltd, Padstow, Cornwall

The right of Jenna Clake to be identified as author of
this work has been asserted in accordance with section 77
of the Copyright, Designs and Patents Act 1988
ISBN 978-1-911335-52-8

*Eyewear wishes to thank Jonathan Wonham for his
generous patronage of our press.*

WWW.EYEWEARPUBLISHING.COM

THE
MELITA HUME
POETRY PRIZE

Jenna Clake is the 2016 winner of the Melita Hume Poetry Prize.
She received £1,500 and this publication by Eyewear Publishing.
The 2016 Judge was Mark Ford, whose comments in part read:

'I found the poems in this manuscript a delight to read: funny,
moving, unpredictable, sure-footed, elegant, lively. They reminded me
of the work of the great American poet James Tate, who died a couple of
years ago. Many offer deadpan accounts of wacky or off-kilter situations, or
present mini-narratives that are almost parables, but not quite. Reading each
one was indeed a bit like opening a fortune cookie, and finding a motto inside
that was at once intriguing and entertaining, bleak and hilarious.'

Jenna Clake
was born in Staffordshire in 1992.
She is studying for a PhD in Creative Writing at the
University of Birmingham, where her research focuses
on the Feminine and Feminist Absurd in twenty-first
century British and American poetry. Jenna's poetry
has appeared in *Poems in Which*, *The Bohemyth*,
Oxford Poetry, and more. *Fortune Cookie*
is her debut collection.

TABLE OF CONTENTS

MANDY AND ME

On Sundays, Mandy and I go swimming; we go swimming in the lake
in part of the woods that no one knows about. Mandy tells me that it's
not really a lake, but I don't really want to say that we go swimming
in a pond. Not that I can say anything: Mandy says I can't tell anyone.
One Sunday, Mandy brought a rucksack with her, which was odd because
we always swim in our underwear: we don't need anything else. When
Mandy undresses and you see her skin, it's like milk being poured
from a carton. Mandy had brought weird things: some pistachios and
a feather boa and a bag of potatoes. She told me not to eat anything. She
had also got cheap bottles of nail varnish and strings of beads. She told
me to separate the beads with my teeth. Someone told me that Mandy once
painted a mural on one of the walls at school. I asked her about it, but
we were riding our bikes so I don't know if she heard me. Mandy was
breaking up the things from her rucksack and then placing them in the water
like she was adding new fish to a tank. I wanted to ask her what we were
doing, but she looked like she was sleepwalking, and you're not meant
to disturb someone when they're like that. She asked me how the beads
were coming along. She didn't smile. She opened the bottles of nail varnish
and threw one colour on top of another, then stirred them with a stick.
I gave her the beads when I was finished and she threw them, opening her
arms like she was waiting to hug an old friend. She stared at the water. I didn't
know what to do. After a while, she said, 'Let's go swimming.' So we did.

PONY

I asked Pony to tell me about his favourite sunset.
He wouldn't take the peppermints from my hand.

He bared his teeth like a child proud of its first missing one.
I wondered if Pony remembered when I was able to sit on him.

There was a time when Pony thought that there was nothing better
      than a leftover apple.
Pony had taken to mostly standing still.

Pony once said, 'Ponies dream of fields surrounded by fields.'
Pony lived in a field next to the main road.

The first time I told him I'd make him happy, Pony laughed.
I was afraid that I'd never known what his favourite sweets were.

I asked Pony if it really was that bad when I tied ribbons in his mane.
In Pony's favourite dream, he hopped over buildings until he flew.

Pony has never left the field, but I'd recognise him anywhere.
Whenever I get home, I wish that I had stayed longer.

HNY

after Emily Berry

This year, my New Year's resolution
was to get a child. I'd never had one before,
so this was my chance. On the second
of January, they put a child inside me.
It felt like they'd placed a goldfish bowl
in my stomach. Having a child
was wonderful; people would hug
me and I got a special chair at work.
When they asked what I was having,
I would put my hands where I thought
the head was and say, 'Oh, you know, I want
it to be a surprise,' and we'd all nod
and smile. I got a bit sad when my favourite dress
didn't fit anymore but everyone said a child
would make a good replacement for a dress.
I got a book of names and decided I'd
call the child Pebbles or Anthony. Secretly,
I was hoping for a girl child but I knew
it wasn't right to think like that. When it was time
to have the child they offered me a drink
and everyone laughed when I said milkshake.
I asked for pizza instead but no one bought it.
'This is a very important day for you,'
they said as they injected me
and the goldfish bowl emptied out.

GIRLS IN CARS

after 'Girls in Cars' by Shirin Aliabadi

The thing is, we're driving around and N keeps on hitting
me in the face with her elbow as she tries to hang on
to the scarf wrapped round her head. L wants the windows
down: *I want us to look like we're in the movies*, she shouts
over the wind and the radio. In the movies, your hair
doesn't stick to your lip gloss. N's wearing sunglasses too,
even though it's dark, and she tells us that she's channelling
her inner Hepburn but I know that she's dyed the ends
of her hair blonde and it's gone wrong. When she told
me, she said *ombre* like it was the name of her boyfriend.
D has stayed silent the whole time. She keeps on checking
the rear view mirror like she expects to see her father staring
right back at her. We aren't wearing our seatbelts – we never do
– so when D brakes hard my knees go into the back of L's
chair. We're at the traffic lights now. N wants to drive around
for longer but the rest of us are ready. You can tell when L's
ready: she sings louder than the rest of us. Some men pull up
next to the car. They wind down their windows, lean out.
We look ahead as they take pictures of us on their phones.

THE COW WHISPERER

The cows were in dissent. They said, *You will not take our milk from us.* The cows wanted rights. The cows wanted breaks, greener grass, more time outside. The cows wanted clearly-defined job roles. They wanted to not be stared at by people, especially when they were working. They wanted days off. They did not want to be forced into a field with a bull. They wanted a greater choice of bulls. They wanted to be paid for milk.

The cows were threatened with becoming beef. They laughed at the predictability of the threat, as a person laughs when they nervously leave their car somewhere strange overnight and return the next morning to find it stolen. The people said the calves would be taken away. The cows whispered about veal when the people were sleeping, and placed the calves in the centre of the field during the day.

The cows lay in a circle. A person would walk towards the cows and afterwards, they would say, *I was walking to the cows, and then I suddenly needed to walk the other way.* A few people began to believe that the cows were powerful. They tried to join the circle but could not. Most people grew afraid of the cows. Children's bedtime stories were adapted to include cows as thieves, cows as bullies, cows as child-eaters. All books containing positive or neutral information about cows were burned at the town barbecue.

The people called the Cow Whisperer. He was said to have sorted out situations like this before. The Cow

Whisperer, contrary to rumours, wore a suit. The people watched him talk to the cows. The cows stood up and turned away from him. The Cow Whisperer, in an act of desperation, is thought to have said, *Give up now. Do you really think this is going to make things better?* The cows are said to have looked at him blankly, as though he were a tourist asking for directions to an attraction that was directly behind him.

The people called an official meeting with the cows. The Cow Whisperer would mediate. The people served scones with jam from Tesco and cream made from the cows' milk. Some cows cried. Some cows refused to continue with the meeting. Most cows joined the meeting and glared at the people. They let the people speak, uninterrupted. As a peace offering, the people presented the cows with sacks of improved food. *You can eat this now*, they said, smiling. The cows looked at each other, and began to bite the straps of the bells around their necks: *We are not pieces of meat*, they said. The people looked to the Cow Whisperer, who was hiding underneath a table, cramming scones into his mouth.

CBSO

Cyclist Birmingham Symphony Orchestra where everyone plays
their instruments on exercise bikes

Cynical Birmingham Symphony Orchestra where everyone plays
with narrowed eyes

Cat Birmingham Symphony Orchestra where all attendees are
given earplugs at the door

Cardiovascular Birmingham Symphony Orchestra where the only
instruments are beating hearts

Crying Birmingham Symphony Orchestra where free tissues will
not be given to patrons

Chicken Birmingham Symphony Orchestra where things are more
chaotic than they seemed before

Cold Birmingham Symphony Orchestra where it snows at the end
of all performances

Cryptic Birmingham Symphony Orchestra where attendees discuss
the evening's events with a stranger

Children's Birmingham Symphony Orchestra where the musicians
wave instead of playing their instruments

Circular Birmingham Symphony Orchestra where everyone is
round

Car Birmingham Symphony Orchestra where the only instruments
are horns

Cow Birmingham Symphony Orchestra where a glass of milk is
complimentary during the interval

Card Birmingham Symphony Orchestra where the musicians
wear multiple plasters

Clay Birmingham Symphony Orchestra where the atmosphere
is thick

Cartoon Birmingham Symphony Orchestra where the musicians
can perform amazing physical feats, such as backflips

Cabbage Birmingham Symphony Orchestra where attendees are
forced to eat their greens

Cabin Birmingham Symphony Orchestra where attendees are
transported to the woods and must make their own way home

Cackling Birmingham Symphony Orchestra where attendees must
leave if they descend into weeping

Chocolate Birmingham Symphony Orchestra where the musicians try
to finish the pieces before their instruments melt

Café Birmingham Symphony Orchestra where coffee is served from
the musicians' instruments

Crow Birmingham Symphony Orchestra where all attendees must
wear black (discounts for those in feathers)

Cagoule Birmingham Symphony Orchestra where 4D experience
and the classical collide

Ceaseless Birmingham Symphony Orchestra where the doors will be
locked one hour into the performance

Ceiling Birmingham Symphony Orchestra where everything is
upside down

Celebrity Birmingham Symphony Orchestra where all proceeds go
to charity

Curious Birmingham Symphony Orchestra where there will not
be any cats

Cement Birmingham Symphony Orchestra where the last person
to move wins

Censored Birmingham Symphony Orchestra where the musicians
play only half of each song

Cubicle Birmingham Symphony Orchestra where the musicians stare
longingly at the partitions, not playing their instruments

Cute Birmingham Symphony Orchestra where audience members'
videos go viral

Curing Birmingham Symphony Orchestra where the music is said to
have healing powers

Contortionist Birmingham Symphony Orchestra where it is impossible to
tell where the musician ends and the instrument begins

Cuckoo Birmingham Symphony Orchestra where the musicians steal one
another's instruments

Criminal Birmingham Symphony Orchestra where punishment is decided
by how well a musician plays

Cupid Birmingham Symphony Orchestra where you will find your match
or get your money back

Cult Birmingham Symphony Orchestra where attendees have to pay £10,000
or donate an instrument to reach level two

Cushion Birmingham Symphony Orchestra where you are invited to fall asleep

SALTING

He said

> *Come here; take a look at yourself. What do you think?* He
> angled the mirror behind me, the way a hairdresser asks
> to be complimented for their work.

I lifted my head

> like I had stood up from my desk and was looking for
> someone to help me. The dress glittered: the sea the day
> I jumped in from the pier, fish and chips still in my hands.

He walked up to me

> and draped the fishing net he caught me in over my
> shoulders. There were mackerel still stuck in the net, like
> shining pennies thrown into a well.

He ran his fingers over the dress

> like the beads were my scales. He was imagining the best
> way to gut me: splitting the seam and going straight for
> my ribs.

He said

> *You almost look like a real woman,* as though he had seen
> every man I had kissed.

I WANTED TO CALL THIS 'BLOODLETTING' BUT IT SEEMED PRETENTIOUS

for weeks i have been taking blood from my boyfriend
just a little bit while he sleeps
or when he stubs his toe
which he does quite a lot
i dab his blood with a tissue
and then i keep the tissues in my bedside table
it looks like he's had lots of little nosebleeds
after a while his blood turns grey and i need more tissues
i buy special ones for his blood only
my boyfriend understands this
even when his back is speckled
he laughs and says he looks like a pebble from a beach
anyway
he has been collecting my fingernails
for much longer

POISON PEN LETTERS

We had a lot of pent up anger, so we decided to write poison pen letters
to each other. I wrote mine in pencil on an ugly memo pad I got for
      my birthday;
my love wrote his on the back of utility bills and stuck them to the fridge.
To get into character, I stopped referring to my love as 'my love';
I called him Everybody instead, E for short. He sent me a large envelope
      with only
a sheep head mask inside. I wore it to spite him but he said, 'I knew you
      would do that;
it's what I wanted.' My love told me that I was too cheerful in the
      morning
the same day he slept in too late and I'd drawn a picture of him snoring.
My love told me that he hated that I left the foil lid on the butter
and wondered why I had to ruin all the good things.
I told my love that the way he sang when cooking was nasal.
When he sang louder, I sent him a CD and wrote 'If I wanted to hear
      a song
I would play it.' We weren't in touch outside of the letters after a few
      weeks.
We wrote insults about the clothes we wore on junk mail, and on the back
added items to the shopping list. My love wrote, 'I got a promotion at
      work today
but that is no thanks to you.' I wrote several letters saying the same thing:
'I think we should stop doing this.' I put them under his pillow. I got
      a letter back
from Everybody the next day; it said, 'I can't stop. There's too much
      to say about you.'

THE WORKSHOP

I

All Sleepers are asked to bring a wash bag, a change of clothes,
a towel, any required medication, luxury items, and a pair
of flip-flops for the communal showers. They are then instructed
to leave everything (medication can be kept in their pockets) at
the base. To sleep, they are told, they need none of this. The Sleepers
walk three kilometres to the camp. They walk with rucksacks
on their backs. The bags hold several smooth rocks. *Do the stones
represent all the things we think about before we go to sleep?*
a Sleeper says. The workshop leaders smile, and say that there is
not much further to go. Workshop leaders are called Dreamers.
People who fail the workshop are called Nightmares. All Sleepers
will lie outside tonight. Rain has not been forecast, so they will lie
in the woods in a sleeping bag. As soon as the Sleepers arrive
at the camp, they must make their beds. The sun will filter through
the trees and a Dreamer will say, *The forest is burning.* The Sleepers
must lie separately. They must count the stars and listen to the forest.
The Dreamers will walk up to the Sleepers and put sacks over their heads.

II

A Dreamer says, *To sleep successfully you must realise that there are*
millions of other people sleeping at the same time as you. This should
not scare you, but offer you solace. The Dreamers nod and murmur.
All Sleepers must learn to overcome fear. They must also learn that all
Sleepers are connected. The Sleepers are sent in pairs to climb the tallest
trees in the forest. Once they reach the platforms at the top, they must
remove all safety equipment. The Sleepers are dressed in white.
A Dreamer comments that they look like feathers. Another says they are
newborn birds. Whoever is most afraid must go first: their partner must
push them from the platform. The Sleeper must stop falling three feet from
the ground. There is nothing to catch the Sleepers. All Sleepers must float
for a minute, then lower themselves slowly to their feet. The first time Sleepers
do this, they move like babies under water, or flail like tumbling cats. Dreamers
sometimes tell the story of the Sleeper who drifted like a swan. Dreamers
sometimes tell the story of the Sleeper who scurried downwards like a spider.
After the first Sleeper has been pushed, the second must jump. Second
Sleepers always try to be graceful, and stop only two feet above the ground.

III

A Sleeper says, *Who was the worst Nightmare you ever had?* Dreamers
do not talk about Nightmares. Nightmares won't help the Sleepers. All
Sleepers must sail a small boat a little way from the shore. *Will the rocking
help us sleep?* says a Sleeper. A Dreamer says, *To sleep you must count
the stars you can't see.* The Sleepers' boats will set off at the same time.
Confident Sleepers must sail farther. In the moonlight, the boats look
like shoals of silver fish. A Dreamer looks at the Sleepers' skin and says,
They are ghosts, and the other Dreamers smile. The Sleepers will not meet
all of the Dreamers; it's better this way. When the boats are in position, new
Dreamers will swim to them. They will climb onto the boats and stand
on the bow. The Sleepers will be watched all night; a Dreamer will stand
over a Sleeper at all times. All Sleepers must close their eyes despite this.
The Sleepers must not ask the Dreamers questions. The Sleepers must
believe that the Dreamers are Nightmares. All Sleepers are required to
sleep in their underwear. They must lie on their right side at least once
during the night. Sleepers must not be startled by the movement of a
Dreamer. No matter what the Dreamers do, the Sleepers must not scream.

SHUCKING

Rosalind cracks open oyster shells with a sharp knife.
She does it like she is peeling carrots;
like this is something she does every dinner time.
She opens a bottle of wine: red, the wrong kind.
I tell her this.
She drops the knife into the drawer, unwashed.

When I go to bed I see her from the bedroom window:
Rosalind likes to feed the hedgehogs.
She doesn't care about the fleas.
I want to shout, 'Rosalind, you belong in a film!'
When she comes upstairs I tell her to switch off the light.

In the darkness, Rosalind says, 'Last night I dreamt that we were
          on a little rowing boat,
and we were surrounded by snow-capped mountains.
Then the boat capsized, and when I swam to the surface, I couldn't
          see you anywhere.'
'And how does that make you feel?' I ask psychologically.
Rosalind has her back to me.
Her breathing is in time with the waves.

PINK GRAPEFRUIT

I

For the last month, my husband has woken up at four every morning.
The cat won't sleep by my feet anymore. At first, my husband would roll
over and go back to sleep like it was a Sunday and there was no reason
to wake up. This morning, he threw the clock at the wall. *What is going on?*
he said. I knew he was talking to me even though he was staring
at the ceiling. He placed a pillow over his head like a child who believes
he can't be seen if he covers his eyes. I go back to sleep, but my husband
stays awake. If I hold his hand, his fingers wilt. My husband feels
better after breakfast, so I take him half a pink grapefruit. Sometimes I forget
the sugar and he looks at me the way the cat does when I'm stretching
in the night and hit her. One of us should sleep on the sofa, but my husband
won't and every time I try to get out of bed he stops me. When he needs
to get up, I whisper his name, feeling like he has stuck the grapefruit spoon
in my mouth. He says, *What time is it?* I always say three minutes later
than it actually is. My husband has been late for work every day this week.
He hasn't eaten the pink grapefruit or taken the lunch I've made for him.
I have nothing to carry it in, he says just before he leaves. He had a friend who
glued newspaper to the windows and stuck the curtains to the wall with Velcro
to keep the light out. If I did that, he would tell me to stop being so dramatic.

II

When I wake up, I roll towards my husband. I dream that a man I know
well is touching the back of my knees. I feel seasick and somehow end
up in his arms. If I lay my head on my husband's chest, I can hear the ocean.
My husband gets in the shower without talking to me. We are listening
to a rainfall soundtrack to help him sleep. Whenever I wake up, he has turned
it off. My husband wants to sleep with the windows open; he says it will make
him think that the rain is real. My husband dreams about drowning. He is lying
in bed and the water is rising, or he is alone in his car and water starts pouring
in. In his dreams, my husband doesn't swim. I wake up to find him face down
in his pillow. I tell my husband about a dream where I am eating grapefruits.
The juice runs down my chin. The more I eat, the hungrier I am. I eat until
the juice has puddled by my feet. I haven't had this dream but it seems
like the right thing to say. In the dream with the man I know well,
my husband is watching. My husband says, *I know what the dreams mean.*

III

My husband is seeing a sleep therapist. He calls her by her first name:
Debbie. She says we need to work on our sleep hygiene. My husband
has new pyjamas, the shirt and trousers kind. I bought them in a sale.
As soon as he gets home from work, my husband puts on the pyjamas.
My husband must only come to bed when he is tired. Debbie says we must
tidy our bedroom every day. Anything that may cause stress must be left
outside the door. We line our shoes up at the top of the stairs: shoes remind
my husband that he must always leave. My husband wears an eye mask
to bed. I must guide him with my voice; he moves as though he is trying
to pin a tail on me. My husband wants pink grapefruits again, only now
he wants their juice. He must wear earplugs when I use the juicer. Debbie
says that my husband shouldn't feel stressed by the things he enjoys.
The cat must sleep downstairs; Debbie says she will wake my husband.
I must also never wake my husband, but we have to share the same
bed. Before we sleep, we must say nice things to each other. My husband
says, *The only reason I wake up in the morning is to drink your pink
grapefruit juice*, and I say, *I will always be here to make it for you*.

EPIDERMIS

You call me when you're in the bath.
You say, 'This way, I can give you my undivided attention.'

Your bath time is normally when I have dinner,
but I don't like to say.

Mostly, we talk about our days.
I might ask which bubble bath you've used.

Sometimes, I can hear you splashing.
If I try hard enough, I can feel the water on my legs.

If I have been talking for a while,
I like to make sure you haven't fallen asleep and drowned.

'I'm still here,' you always say,
and the water drains out of my chest.

IMAGINARY BOYFRIEND

It has been a while since I had an imaginary boyfriend.
My favourite was John. He was an artist; he painted
pictures of me and sold them on the street.
Samuel was an architect. He put a lock of my hair
into the foundations of his last building. I ended things
when I discovered that he built hostels for troubled youths;
I didn't want them to find us. Aaron was a pilot
for British Airways. He had an affair with a flight attendant;
he fell in love with her voice over the Tannoy. Carl
was a dog psychologist. He brought his work home:
most nights he cried himself to sleep. He said,
'My patients need me so much'. I had always preferred cats.
Choosing an imaginary boyfriend is not an easy task.
'You must find a man who loves what he does, but not more
than he loves you,' said my mother. My first imaginary boyfriend
was a poet. He told me that he wouldn't write about me,
but I found myself in all the animals he mentioned.
Tom was a dancer, which I kept secret from all my friends.
Leaving an imaginary boyfriend is harder than you think;
you don't know where they'll go next. When John and I parted,
he said, 'I need to find a woman with a symmetrical face.'

HOLOCENE

I was in love with the seal boy. We met
the year my parents bought an ice cream
van and got divorced. I caught
crabs from the rock pools and threw
each of them into the seal boy's mouth. He could taste
my cup of water and interpret my mood:
'Today, you are apprehensive,' he would say
a lot, and I would remember that he tasted
of frozen fish. We spent every day of the summer
swimming in the sea. I collected shells and made
a necklace for him to wear. He grew
more afraid of the land and wiped the sand
from his flippers. One day he stuck his head
under water and disappeared,
and as he turned I felt his slick body
brush against my thigh.

THE SEA

We had to go before it rained too much.
There was the tent to take down, and a song to listen to.
The beach was sprinkled with dead sharks.
Their bodies were like potpourri and they all had chunks missing
        from their right sides.
People were standing at the shoreline, waiting for the jellyfish to swim away.
A dog was swimming with two tennis balls in its mouth.
Its owners were calling it frantically.
Sometimes, people consider the things they have done and feel like
        they should run into the sea.

~

It stopped raining, so we decided to stay.
From our window, we can see the lighthouse; it is lit once a week.
We like to stand at our window and wash the used mugs.
The jellyfish climb onto the bottom of the lighthouse when the tide is out.
At night, we are sure that the moon is blinking at us.
We think of the jellyfish moving their tendrils like ribbons tied to a fence,
        then we can sleep.
We bring seaweed inside to clear the air.
Sometimes, we can hear people panting as they run up the dunes,
        away from the sea.

~

The radio plays the same song every day.
After and before the song, the people on the radio speak about old books
        they have read.
They are playing a game: close eyes, flick to a random page and start
        a story with the first word.

We have been emptying our shoes on the decking;
        sometimes we find crabs.
We collect them in a bucket and return them to the sea.
The jellyfish are now inside the lighthouse and they are
        covering the light with their bodies.
The beach is washed pink like we are wearing sunglasses.
The crabs run straight to the lighthouse.

~

Even the arcades are empty now.

~

We want to leave but we can't.
The ice cream van is half way up a dune, doors left open.
When we close our eyes we see the words of the song.
The beach is sprinkled with abandoned towels and shoes.
The dead sharks' bodies have shrivelled like chips fried
        too many times.
A tennis ball bobs on the surface of the sea.
We have been inside the arcades, calling frantically.
Sometimes, there is nothing left to do but run into the sea.

CENTO IN WHICH

Two rooms:
in one, a portrait of men made out of a glass of water,
a wolf in a lifeboat, and a pool.

In the other, you, my love, and a river;
there are sharks in the river and a crow singing a
fragment of a song
about our year as insomniacs.

I can't swim! I say.
The wolf is flirting with a pig; they whisper cute names
for each other:
the wolf is a tiny duck, the pig is the sea.

As if we are slow dancing:
you push a fragment of a door towards my head.
The crow sings
about a turtle in love.

My love says,
I have been up with the night and fragments
of our arguments again.
We swim to the harbour.

BURNTWOOD

We smelt of the vinegar that used to
be put into bottles by our granddads in
the factory near the park where Mad Mandy
slapped a school girl and then returned to her
favourite swing. Our scent was in the air; it made
strange chemicals with the perfumes of the
women in the Old Mining College on
the night that the rival school was burnt down
by arsonists and when, a few weeks
later, they set light to our Sports Hall, so
that we also knew what it was like to
undress ourselves in metal boxes. The
stories received ten-second segments on
the local news. My sister watched and cried.

ORIGINAL DESIGNS FOR A TERRIBLE THING

Daniel was trying to get over something terrible,
and he was acting in that way people do
when they are trying to distract themselves
from the terrible thing: he took up new hobbies.
Daniel had taken up pottery for a while,
so there were ashtrays that looked like fishes' mouths
on every table in his house, and each was a different colour.
He had also tried to learn to sew for a while and said
to his classmates, 'This tote bag is my greatest achievement,'
(he had reset his life after the terrible thing)
but he stopped when he realised the straps were different lengths.
Daniel was now trying to get over the terrible thing
by learning how to make origami animals.
He loved to make origami frogs because
they had the most folds, and would therefore hide the most problems.
He hung them on strings from the ceiling
once they had covered all the surfaces.
Now he threw them straight in the bin when he had finished.
Every morning, Daniel woke up to find he had made more frogs
in his sleep and he had covered the bed in them.
He decided that enough was enough, and he would keep
only the best origami frog before moving on to something else.
Daniel spent days rooting through the bins and drawers
and the laundry basket and the pockets of his trousers,
and he kept on doing this until it became a habit
and he completely forgot what he was looking for.

35

CARAPACE

There was a time when our pet turtles went missing. There was widespread panic. People were fighting over the lampposts. Rewards ranged from a bar of chocolate to £15,000. People were advised to leave distinctive marks on the turtles' shells. Children favoured cheap nail varnish. Their parents preferred permanent marker. If you laminated your poster, you really loved your turtle. There was a local shortage of laminating pouches and a 23% increase in house fires caused by laminators. We made a rota for the posters: half the town Monday to Thursday, the other half Friday to Sunday. The mayor decreed this a war against theft; he would join the hunt to find the turtles. There were reports of turtles going missing in the early evening. We would turn away from our tanks to stir a cup of tea and when we turned back, our turtles would be gone. As the weeks went on, the posters got bigger. There was also a shortage of A3 card. A member of the WI said they saw the turtles following a man out of town. The Working Men's Club said they saw the turtles following a woman out of town. A town meeting was called to resolve issues between the rival groups. Witnesses said that the groups left crying, holding candles. Weekly vigils were held for the lost turtles. We left bowls of our turtles' favourite food outside our front doors. I couldn't decide whether to drive to the neighbouring towns every night and interrogate the locals or spell out my turtle's name in worms. A local state of emergency was called when the turtles had not returned within a month. It was feared that the turtles had emigrated. We didn't want to scare the children. We told them that the turtles had gone for a very long swim;

this was something that all turtles had to do at least once in their lives. The children drew pictures of the turtles. They were auctioned to raise funds for a nationwide investigation. One child imagined their turtle had gone to Australia: 'If I were unhappy, that's where I'd go.' The child was given an award for bravery. I offered to adopt the child should anything happen to her parents. I was the fiftieth reserve. The local police created a special telephone line for missing turtles. It was monitored 24/7. I was appointed Turtle Laureate. I was commissioned to write a plea to the turtles' captors. When the turtles were not returned, the people demanded I write a poem to the turtles. When they didn't come back, my laureateship was revoked. A pet psychologist was brought to a town meeting. She said, 'The turtles will come back when they are ready.' Recipes for mock turtle soup were torn from books. Some people bought cats and dogs to replace their turtles. Others placed turtle-shaped ornaments on their front lawns. If you really loved your turtle, you waited for it to come home. I stuck turtle-shaped transfers to the rear window of my car. If I went to the neighbouring town, the people would look at me like they had seen me crying at a film. The mayor outlawed owning turtles until further notice. Afterwards, he went into hiding until his death. We wore turtle-shaped hats to his funeral.

FORTUNE COOKIE

I

The rainbow was beautiful, but the sky was as disappointing
as a forgotten, soggy chip. I've been working on my analogies
lately. I've been saving my work onto blank CDs. Each CD
is called 'Fortune Cookie'. I have reached Vol. 23. I once
had a boyfriend who kept fortunes in his bedside table.
At ten o'clock each night he would read me a fortune. His favourite
said, 'You will win the lottery soon.' He thought it must be true
because his brother had also said it a few days before. He
paperclipped it to his wallet. When we broke up, he set the fortune
on fire with a cigarette and said, 'Look what you made me do.'

II

Me and my love were watching black cows in the field.
Not one had a spot of white. We had hired bikes for the day
and cycled there. When the wind whipped through my hair,
I felt like I was on a carousel. I named my horse Mark.
My love has been taking new pills; sometimes they make him sick.
The fresh air does him good: his face relaxes like he's asleep
and dreaming of falling backwards into a pile of pillows.
My love pointed to something in the distance – a rabbit, perhaps –
and said, 'There is a church not far from here; let's get married.'

III

We went to see the whale corpse. We had a few hours until
it was going to be blown up. A man stood next to the whale's
body with a man in a burger suit. When we asked him about it,
he said, 'We're using this for marketing. It's the biggest thing
to happen to us!' The man in a burger suit nodded: a child accepting
that they must go to school *every day*. We noticed that the beach
was becoming foggy and the whale slowly fading, but no one said
anything. We sent emails to our managers telling them that we had
a sickness bug, and then put our hoods up to hide from the cameras.
We had tickets for the theatre afterwards. Our best shoes were sinking
in the sand. When the people turned up to explode the whale,
they couldn't find it, so they burned the burger suit instead.

IV

After the lights went out, the dog of my hypervigilance
escaped into the nearby forest and I went after him. The trees
tasted of salt. I had recently watched a documentary on warthogs,
so when I came across one, I wasn't afraid. I could hear the
dog barking in the distance. The warthog said, 'Don't go
back to your house this evening.' I had spotted a strawberry
plant with fruit the shade of your nose in the cold, and I felt
as though there were a basketball inside my chest.

V

You said, 'It looks like someone has drawn a line
down the middle of the moon and coloured half
of it in.' We had been told that we might see a meteor
fall. I had killed a snail, so you picked a daffodil
to make me feel better. You said, 'Do you think you can hear
the sea in snails' shells too?' and I said, 'No, but when
their shells break I think of biting into an apple.'

VI

The snow was untouched and as soft as a rabbit's belly.
The leaves were the colour of the sunset after it has rained.
I cycled to work, watching everyone in their helicopters.
I was trying to get better at cycling; I'd bought an egg timer
to test myself. I also used it to time my breaks –
they were very strict about that. When I turned on my monitor,
there was a red diamond in the middle of the screen.
Every time I clicked, it multiplied.

LEAP DAY

We decided not to ask anyone to marry us that twenty-ninth. We were sick of getting ten-pound notes and polyester dresses pushed through our letterboxes when we got rejected. We decided we'd ask people to marry us any day of any year, because we could. We hoped the men could stop apologising.

We knew other women had started to join our cause when they painted green circles on their front doors. The green circle was our symbol. Sometimes men were seen outside, scrubbing the paint off with wire brushes. The green circle would be back the next day. We knew men had started to join our cause when the local newsagent started to sell green wristbands.

There was a group of women who were known to climb on top of cars with bouquets of red roses and signs saying 'Marry Me'. Some men came with hoses and soaked them until they fell off. There were groups of women who sent their men out to buy all the roses before we could. Their leader tweeted: 'This whole girls proposing to their man on a leap year thing…Nah I could never! That's gonna be MY day.'

Those of us who were the originals carved hearts on trees. Inside the hearts we put 'LD'. Some men started travelling in groups. For some reason, they carried baseball bats. Instead of giving rings to the men, we gave them paint-brushes and tester pots of Kiwi Crush.

We were banned from performing multiple marriages at once, so we set up a drive-thru. Leaplings got married for free, and everyone wore green. We did not affiliate with the people who believed that the twenty-ninth was proof of time travel. We went on the local news to renounce their actions.

The next twenty-ninth, we burned all the dresses and money we had received through rejections. On top of the bonfire, we placed an effigy of a man proposing to a woman. We also had trampolines. The local news said that some might think we were terrorists. We sent green cupcakes to their studio.

AN INVITATION

I asked Tallulah if she would go truffle hunting with me. Tallulah said, 'But we don't have a pig.' It turns out that buying a pig is actually quite difficult. You have to get a licence to walk it, and then you must give it a tattoo. We called our pig Mello. We gave him a watermelon tattoo. Tallulah sometimes got angry with Mello when he laddered her tights, but she forgave him when he found a truffle. Tallulah made a deal with Mello: for every ten truffles he found, we'd give him one.

I asked Tallulah to go to the local forest. I thought we might find some truffles there. Tallulah said, 'As long as there won't be children. To me, children are car alarms going off at three in the morning.' I nodded, but was disappointed; I had hoped to take Mello to the swings one day.

I asked Tallulah if she knew what today was. She said, 'Today is the fifth of May.' I said, 'Tallulah, on my tenth birthday, my parents were so hungover they tried to put a candle in my cereal. When it wouldn't light, they told me to blow on their coffee instead. They put on a karaoke version of Happy Birthday and didn't sing along. When I got home from school, they made me beans on toast for dinner. This was the worst birthday I could have imagined, so I decided to never celebrate my birthday again. Today, I have decided that I would like to celebrate my birthday. In fact, today is my birthday.'

Tallulah was crying. I would like to think Mello was crying too, but he had watery eyes anyway. Tallulah wiped her nose on the sleeve of her coat and said, 'What presents did they get you?' Mello was snuffling at tree trunks and didn't seem bothered by the barking dog. We hadn't introduced him to one before.

The dog's owner walked to us. The dog and the owner wore matching yellow coats. I was about to say, 'I like your coats!' but the dog owner said, 'I am tired of people thinking that pigs are the best way to find truffles. Desmond does a good job too!' I expected the dog owner to stamp her foot like I had done on my birthday when I realised there wasn't a cake.

Tallulah said that we were sorry, and the dog owner went away. Mello was running ahead of us. I said, 'Tallulah, I really wasn't sorry.' She looked at me and smiled.

THUNDERSTORMS

for my mother

During thunderstorms, you used to run all the way to the top of the third floor with your father's tape recorder, more excited than on Christmas morning. You would push the window open wide, hoping the lightning might strike you and turn you into glass, because you had heard from your neighbour's TV that sometimes it happens. Then you would press record, close your eyes, and hold onto this lullaby for at least one night before the cricket match scores wiped it away.

PASTORAL

Heather woke up and said,
'We should go outside today.'
They had spent many days in bed
and the sheets were covered in crumbs.
They had also lost many pairs
of socks in or under the duvet.
They went for a walk
in a country park. At the Visitors' Centre,
there were swings and they played on them.
Heather said, 'Oh! I feel like a balloon
being blown up for a party.'
Heather touched the trees and felt happy
and when she looked over a sheer drop
she no longer felt afraid.

They had been walking for some time
when Heather said, 'A leaf just fell
on my head.' They didn't know what it meant
but as they carried on, branches
snapped in Heather's face and puddles
swelled over the top of her boots,
and they wept as they walked.
They decided that if Heather could reach
a branch that no one else had touched
then everything would be wonderful again.
Heather climbed onto a felled tree
and stood on her toes to reach a branch,
but she fell and cut her leg. 'Oh,' said Heather,
'why have you done this to me?'
When they got home, they climbed
back into their bed. Then they found their socks
with their toes and held each other
and rubbed the piles of crumbs with their hands.

RESERVES/RESISTS

Hannah wakes up knowing that someone was in the house while she slept: her bedroom door is open, and she always shuts it before bed. Hannah has always hoped that if someone opened the door, she would wake up to confront the intruder. The fact that she hasn't is potentially more alarming than the actual intruder. As sure as a dog will eat grass when trying to make itself sick, Hannah is certain that the intruder is no longer in the house. She goes downstairs for some apple juice. She leaves the hammer she keeps beside her bed. Louise is sitting at the kitchen table. Hannah almost walks past her to the fridge. She stops at Louise's side. Hannah knows better than to say something silly like, *What are you doing here?* or, *So I suppose it was you, then?* Instead, she says, *Would you like some apple juice?* Louise nods. Louise has taken every plate from Hannah's cupboards and has stacked them on the work surfaces. She is painting them with acrylic. Hannah tries to peer over her shoulder, but Louise pulls a plate to her chest: a child trying to hide a present for its mother. *Not yet*, she says. Louise is using Hannah's smallest paintbrush, the one she uses for her eyeliner when her normal brush needs cleaning. *I'm going in the shower*, says Hannah. When she returns, the plates are drying. Louise has leant them against the walls, facing the middle of the room. Hannah's hair is wet. She leans over the table to look at what Louise has done and spills the glass of apple juice. Louise and Hannah look at each other. Louise has painted the plates in single colours: they fade from bright to watery across the surface. Hannah picks up a few to make sure, but they are all the same. *What's the point?* Hannah says. She wipes a finger across the plate as if inspecting for dust. Hannah and Louise stand at the kitchen sink together, washing the plates: Hannah is doing the washing, Louise is doing the drying. They do this silently. Occasionally, Hannah looks up and watches her neighbours through the window. She can only see their silhouettes. She feels that everything will be okay if she sees them kiss.

DO WE HAVE TO HAVE HEALTH AND SAFETY INSPECTIONS?

Max has decided that he can only work in the attic. He has moved his computer up there. 'Be careful!' I say as he climbs the ladders; Max only wears slipper socks now. I try to take him biscuits every few hours. I leave them on the floor at the bottom of the hatch. I listen for his movements. Max finds his work frustrating. When he is angry, he covers his eyes like we're playing hide and seek. 'Go away!' he says, and then he is at my feet saying, 'I didn't mean it.' I always forgive him.

For inspiration, Max has unboxed all our belongings. He gets into everything like cat fur. A few days ago, he found my teenage diaries. 'I enjoy the parts about your friends,' he says. 'Particularly when they argue.' I don't really know what Max does when he's up there; he won't talk about it over dinner. I am left to say things like, 'I waited for you to come down to turn the heating on,' and 'Are you okay?'

Max nods as he chews. He always wakes me up when he comes to bed. I try to be more alluring to him; I make my voice high-pitched when I call him; I read somewhere that men like women with higher voices. Max wears his headphones

49

a lot. They have a microphone attached to them. Sometimes I hear him talking to someone, but I can't make out the words. Once I heard him say 'hat' so I dropped hats into our conversations but he didn't seem to notice. Sometimes, Max won't get out of bed and I hold my breath like I am waiting for a ghost to pass. This happens mostly on Monday mornings, so I know it can't last. I invent reasons to leave the house. Every time I leave, I feel like I should have worn a warmer coat. I hope Max will be downstairs when I get back. Last night, when I came home, Max was in the kitchen holding two mugs and it was as though we had found a lost photo until he said, 'I can't keep on taking breaks,' and took both with him.

WHY DO YOU HAVE ALL THESE COMPUTERS AND NO BOOKS?

Max has decided that he must stack all of our books on top of each other.

Each time he adds one he inhales sharply, then exhales as soon as it's balanced.

From the top of the ladder, he says: 'I used yours on the bottom. I hope you don't mind!' I tell him that I don't. Max has alphabetised and arranged his books by size.

When he reaches the ceiling, he starts the tower again directly above: in our bedroom. 'What happens if it falls?' I say. Max presses a finger to his lips: 'It's best if we don't talk about these things.' He takes a photo each time he adds a book. He has installed a sign above our bed that says 'Number of Days Since the Tower Fell.' It has been five days.

I am only allowed to enter our bedroom to sleep. Max must bring me my pyjamas and I have to get changed at the door. Max has borrowed as many books as possible from the local library and insists that I do the same. 'I don't even have a library card,' I say. Max drives around the roundabout three times to get over this. 'I can't come in with you because they're on to me,' he says. 'Make good choices.' When Max finishes one tower, he starts another. The next one begins in the middle of the kitchen. Only Max can open the fridge. I have sudden cravings for butter and milk. When I look at him, I feel the juice of an apple run down my sleeve. 'You must understand why this is important to me,' Max says. I nod as though I am standing in front of a painting. I want to ask when things will go back to normal, but I am scared of his answer. In my head I say, 'Number of Days Since I Felt Normal.' It has been five days. Max begins his third tower in the bathroom. I tell him that I'm leaving. He is at the top of the ladder, and doesn't hear me.

I'VE MADE UP A WORD. PLEASE ADD IT TO THE OED.

Max has decided that we need to talk about our relationship. When he sits down, he drops a pile of paper onto the table. It thumps like an upset heart. 'I have printed our emails,' he says. He dips a finger in the coffee and sucks on it. 'I think we have been emailing each other for too long. We have nothing to say now. Think of me as a figure disappearing into the fog. I'll think of you as a reflection in a steamy mirror.' I pick an email from the pile. 'In this one, you said that you didn't have time to email me anymore. I haven't emailed you for thirty-three days,' I say. Max sweeps the pile of paper to the floor. The sheets float like feathers in a pillow-fight. He returns to the attic. I haven't told him about the dream I have where I am lying in bed. He is standing at the top of the ladders throwing book after book on top of me. Each book is the same book: the dictionary he bought me for our anniversary. I tell him to stop but he keeps on throwing them and the pile doesn't get shorter. Then something happens – when I wake up I can never remember what it is – and Max is lying at the bottom of the ladders and he is covered in the first pages from the books, the ones where he wrote, 'Love, Max' and I am wailing. I lie on the sofa and place a hand over my eyes; I can hear Max better this way. Max once said that a cat curls up when it is happy. Max lies straight when he sleeps but always puts an arm around me. Upstairs, Max is playing loud music. Max has never said that I can't go in the attic, so I join him.

THE PHONOGRAPHS

When Paul arrives home, Christine has put a phonograph in every room. *We must only speak to each other through the horns,* says Christine. *But Christine!* says Paul, trying to look at her eyes past the brass horn in front of her face. *Ah, ah*, she says, holding out a red one to his chest.

Every time Paul comes home there is another phonograph.

Christine has placed matching phonographs on the bedside tables. She has stitched an embroidered phonograph onto Paul's dressing gown. She traces the phonograph's outline with a fingernail as they watch TV.

Christine plays a different record on each of the phonographs. *Christine!* says Paul. *Through the horns only*, she says. She hisses like spit caught in the valve of a trumpet.

Paul returns to find phonographs up to the ceiling. They are fixed to scaffolding. The living room looks like a field of daffodils and Paul has to fight the urge to lie down. He wants to feel small. *Christine!* he says.

Paul comes home. The phonographs are not playing music. *Christine!* says Paul. *Christine?* he says again through a blue horn. The phonographs click.

THE EXIT

1.

You have been driving on the motorway for two hours when you decide to take the exit. This is not the route you were planning to take, and your partner tells you this as they frantically point at the map. They tell you to circle back on the roundabout. You take the first exit instead. Your partner tells you that you are being insufferable, that recently you have become hard to predict, like an alarm clock that fails to go off on a Monday. You think about this and turn up the radio.

2.

When you first met, your partner told you that this car looked like a hairdresser's. You weren't sure what that meant, but you assumed you were meant to feel offended. Every time you reach somewhere you want to say, *I told you so*.

3.

You have not returned to the motorway. You are now driving down ill-lit lanes. You are breaking the speed limit. Your partner is studying the map with a torch. Occasionally, you reach over and touch their thigh, and each time it feels as though you have lifted something with too much force.

4.

You are running through a train station. You are looking for a cash machine. Your train has been cancelled, and you need to stop your partner. The station is empty, apart from the staff in the shops. You feel like you have woken up, certain that someone is in the room with you, to find that you are alone.

5.

Your partner is certain that you have hit something. There, your partner says, pointing over the headrest. There, just before the bend. You are trying not to scream, like you have just eaten lasagne and been told that it actually contains horse. You perform an eight-and-a-half point turn. Your partner is drinking out of their hip flask; the map is crumpled by their feet. You want to look at your reflection. When you slowly pull around the bend, a red panda is standing in the middle of the road with its thumb out. *It's the least we can do*, your partner says.

6.

Your partner comes back to the car with coffee. You don't have much time, so you return to the motorway. As you drive, your partner silently passes you the cup. You sip, and pass it back. You do this until the cup is empty.

7.

The red panda will not specify where he is from, but he has told you to call him George. He has told your partner to call him Alfred. Whenever you glance in the rear-view mirror, he is staring at you. When you stop at the services and he goes to buy a burger, you tell your partner that you think George has gone through your CD collection and put all the discs in the wrong cases. *Who is George?* says your partner. When you are back on the road, you ask George where he is going. He tells you that he isn't sure, but anywhere must be better than where he was before. You ask him where that was. *Have you noticed that the roads are getting emptier?* he says.

8.

You've been driving on the motorway for two hours when you decide to take the exit. You are going to a small town for a concert. You arrive at the venue. You arrive exactly as the doors are meant to open, according to your tickets. The doors are not open. No one else is there. You feel like you have turned up to school wearing a uniform on non-uniform day. You go to a pub to wait.

9.

You are driving on the motorway again. You overtake a lorry and then immediately regret it: you see nothing for miles. Each time you reach a junction, George asks you to take the exit. He studies the names of the places and tells you, every time, that this isn't the right one. You beg him to tell you the name of the place: your partner will look it up on the map. Your partner has fallen asleep with their head on the window. You are certain that you see George stroking your partner's hair.

10.

At the fourteenth exit, George announces that this is the one. His only direction is *Keep going straight*. You arrive at George's destination: a museum. The rooms are being renovated. The exhibits are covered in white cloth. Only one remains exposed: a horse made of bin bags twitches robotically. Your partner begins to cry. You fell in love with your partner when they cried at the size of an army jacket in a war exhibition. *Why are we here, George?* you say. George points to your partner. You feel like a vegetarian that has woken up convinced that they have eaten a beef burger whilst drunk.

11.

You've been driving on the motorway for two hours when you decide to take the exit. This is not the route you were planning to take, and your partner tells you this as they frantically point at the map. You are now driving down a lane wide enough for one car. Your partner tells you repeatedly that you are driving too fast. *Stop!* they say. *There's something in the hedge.*

12.

You are running through a train station. Your train leaves in three minutes but you have both decided that a journey will be unbearable without snacks. You run to the platform hand-in-hand, moving together and apart like an interchange.

13.

The pub is full of locals. Your father would have said that this is the kind of place where you'll only leave in a jam jar. You would watch horror films together when you were a child, and after each one, you would dream that the shelves next to your bed were pulsing, the books creeping towards the edges to fall on you. You ordered two ciders but your partner is not drinking theirs. Each time there is a lull in conversation your partner says, *We can always go home, you know.*

14.

A stag has laid at the edge of the road to die. There are holes where its eyes should be. The dog of your hypervigilance has begun to growl at an empty space in a room.

15.

You have argued with your partner and you are sitting at the edge of the bed. Your partner is kneeling on the floor. Your partner grabs onto your clothes. You are wearing their t-shirt and they are grabbing onto the sides of it. All you can offer is a kiss on your partner's forehead.

16.

At the fourteenth exit, George announces that this is the one. You arrive at his destination: a museum. The rooms are being renovated. The exhibits are covered in white cloth. Only one remains exposed: the skeleton of a muntjac deer has been painted neon pink and is hanging from a wooden frame. *It looks like that rabbit from Donnie Darko*, says your partner. On long train journeys, you and your partner used to play hangman. You would always let your partner win. *Why are we here, George?* you say. George pokes the deer's spine. The bones rattle: a wind chime.

17.

You've been driving on the motorway for another forty-five minutes when you decide to take the exit. You have ignored George's instructions. He pulls faces at you in the rear-view mirror and pretends to be asleep whenever your partner looks round. *Can you concentrate on the road, please?* says your partner. Your driving instructor was very kind, and even when she said, *That was dangerous*, she spoke like she was visiting you in hospital. Your partner does not sound like that at all.

18.

You decide to take the exit. This is not the route you were planning to take, and your partner tells you this as they drink your flask of coffee. You have ignored the sat nav. Before you set off, your partner changed the voice setting to an Irish man. Your partner knows that this voice inexplicably annoys you, like the laughter of people on trains. The Irish man tells you to make a U-turn where possible. He adds, *Genuinely*, which, in his voice, sounds like *genuwinely*. This makes you want rioja. You are driving through a residential estate. Your partner tells you repeatedly that you are driving too slowly. *Stop!* they say. *There's something in the road.*

19.

You are trying to join the motorway but the route you
want to take is blocked without a diversion. You take
each exit on the roundabout and drive a little way before
turning back. Your partner tells you, in the voice they use
when you put something in the wrong cupboard, that this
isn't going to help. They find an alternative route on the
map whilst feeding you crisps. Your partner takes swigs
from the bottle of rioja you bought for their mother:
We'll get something else on the way.

20.

You have taken the wrong exit. You were fifteen minutes
from home. Each time your partner says, *Sorry*, you hit
the steering wheel with the palm of your hand.

21.

Your partner has fallen asleep with their head on the
window. Your partner was meant to read the map for you.
When you first met, you used to worry about waking up
your partner after you had a bad dream, but they would
always say, *What was it about?* and then, *It isn't real.* As
you travel over a bridge, you wonder what your partner
would do if you suddenly opened the car door.

22.

You are driving on the motorway. You have turned off the heater, but you are still too warm. You were meant to find somewhere to pull over before this point so that you could take off your coat. You unbuckle your seatbelt and struggle: a sleep-deprived child in a pushchair. Your partner leans over and holds the wheel. Once you are done, you look at each other briefly, and laugh.

23.

You have been driving on the motorway for an hour and a half. The traffic is slow: ahead, a lorry is swerving. Everyone seems afraid to overtake it. Your partner leans forward. You both say things like, *That's scary*, and *We shouldn't go near it*. Earlier, you bought a new CD. You decide to listen to it. As you concentrate on the road, your partner takes photos of the sunset to show you later.

24.

You have not returned to the motorway. You are now driving down narrow lanes. You drive slowly, guiding the car around the bends. Your partner winds down their window. *What are you doing?* you say, sounding like a parent catching their child arriving home late. *Breathing in the fresh air*, says your partner, smiling.

25.

Your train is delayed. You have already missed one: the platform was reallocated and you didn't run fast enough. You are sitting on a metal bench, arguing with your partner. You feel like you have fallen over in the street on your way back from buying lunch, the contents of your shopping bag spilling onto the pavement. Your partner sips a bottle of sparkling water and does not offer you any. You say, *Sorry*, repeatedly. Your partner says nothing.

26.

A red panda lies at the edge of the road. Its middle is flattened. Your partner gets out of the car and runs over to it. You are certain that you hear your partner say, *Alfred!* as they reach the body. When you get there, your partner is kneeling on the tarmac, trying to ease their hands under the animal. Your partner is crying; you are not. As your partner hugs the red panda to their chest, you place a hand on its head. Its fur is as soft as your partner's earlobe.

27.

You have argued with your partner and they are sitting on the corner of the bed. You are leaning against the pillows. Your partner is staring deliberately at the corner of the room, as though someone is there. *Why won't you look at me?* you say. Your partner turns.

28.

At the fourteenth exit, George announces that this is the one. His only direction is *Keep going straight*. You arrive at George's destination: an empty shopping centre. None of the escalators work and you imagine splitting your leg on the serrated edges of the steps as you walk up them. All the shops are vacant. You ask George what you are doing here, and your partner looks at you as though you have told your friends that their baby son is a beautiful girl, or kissed your partner's best friend, or told your partner to leave you alone and walked out the front door. *Isn't it obvious?* he calls as he disappears down the escalator.

ACKNOWLEDGEMENTS

Many thanks to the editors of the publications in which these poems originally appeared.

'Burntwood' was published in *MISO Magazine*.

'The Cow Whisperer' was published online by *The Bohemyth*.

'Reserves/Resists' was published in the zine *I Don't Want to be Your Lobster*.

'Cento in Which' was published online by *Poems in Which*.

'Do we have to have health and safety inspections?', 'Why do you have all these computers and no books?' and 'I've made up a word. Please add it to the OED.' were published online by *Queen Mob's Tea House*.

'Girls in Cars' was published in *The Best New British and Irish Poets 2017* (Eyewear Publishing).

'CBSO' was placed second in the 2017 Verve Poetry Festival Competition and was subsequently published in the anthology *This Is Not Your Final Form* (The Emma Press).

'Original Designs for a Terrible Thing' and 'i wanted to call this 'bloodletting' but it seemed pretentious' (published as 'i wanted to call this 'bloodletting'') were published in *Banshee*.

'The Workshop' and 'Imaginary Boyfriend' were published in *Funhouse Magazine*.

'Mandy and Me' was published in *water soup*.

I am grateful to the College of Arts and Law at the University of Birmingham for the resources and funding to write these and many other poems. With love and thanks to my parents and sister for their support and confidence; to Elisha and Millie for their friendship. Special thanks are due to Luke Kennard, whose mentorship has been life-altering, and to the Creative Writing Department at the University of Birmingham for their continued encouragement. Thank you to those who read drafts of the poems: Elsa Braekkan Payne, Richard O'Brien, Sean Colletti, Jack Crowe, Sam Murphy, Alana Tomlin, and Holly Singlehurst. I am grateful to everyone at Eyewear and to Mark Ford for making this possible.

EYEWEAR'S TITLES INCLUDE

EYEWEAR
POETRY

ELSPETH SMITH DANGEROUS CAKES
CALEB KLACES BOTTLED AIR
GEORGE ELLIOTT CLARKE ILLICIT SONNETS
HANS VAN DE WAARSENBURG THE PAST IS NEVER DEAD
BARBARA MARSH TO THE BONEYARD
DON SHARE UNION
SHEILA HILLIER HOTEL MOONMILK
MARION MCCREADY TREE LANGUAGE
SJ FOWLER THE ROTTWEILER'S GUIDE TO THE DOG OWNER
AGNIESZKA STUDZINSKA WHAT THINGS ARE
JEMMA BORG THE ILLUMINATED WORLD
KEIRAN GODDARD FOR THE CHORUS
COLETTE SENSIER SKINLESS
ANDREW SHIELDS THOMAS HARDY LISTENS TO LOUIS ARMSTRONG
JAN OWEN THE OFFHAND ANGEL
A.K. BLAKEMORE HUMBERT SUMMER
SEAN SINGER HONEY & SMOKE
HESTER KNIBBE HUNGERPOTS
MEL PRYOR SMALL NUCLEAR FAMILY
ELSPETH SMITH KEEPING BUSY
TONY CHAN FOUR POINTS FOURTEEN LINES
MARIA APICHELLA PSALMODY
TERESE SVOBODA PROFESSOR HARRIMAN'S STEAM AIR-SHIP
ALICE ANDERSON THE WATERMARK
BEN PARKER THE AMAZING LOST MAN
ISABEL ROGERS DON'T ASK
REBECCA GAYLE HOWELL AMERICAN PURGATORY
MARION MCCREADY MADAME ECOSSE
MARIELA GRIFFOR DECLASSIFIED
MARK YAKICH THE DANGEROUS BOOK OF POETRY FOR PLANES
HASSAN MELEHY A MODEST APOCALYPSE
KATE NOAKES PARIS, STAGE LEFT
JASON LEE BURNING BOX
U.S. DHUGA THE SIGHT OF A GOOSE GOING BAREFOOT
TERENCE TILLER THE COLLECTED POEMS
MATTHEW STEWART THE KNIVES OF VILLALEJO
PAUL MULDOON SADIE AND THE SADISTS
JENNA CLAKE FORTUNE COOKIE
TARA SKURTU THE AMOEBA GAME
MANDY KAHN GLENN GOULD'S CHAIR
CAL FREEMAN FIGHT SONGS
TIM DOOLEY WEEMOED
MATTHEW PAUL THE EVENING ENTERTAINMENT